Kid's Library of Space Exploration

The Space Shuttle Program

Kid's Library of Space Exploration

Becoming an Astronaut

Deep-Space Probes

ISS: The International Space Station

Missions to Mars

Private Space Exploration

Rocket Technology

Space Telescopes

The Space Shuttle Program

Traveling to the Moon

Kid's Library of Space Exploration

The Space Shuttle Program

Kim Etingoff

VILLAGE EARTH PRESS

Kid's Library of Space Exploration: The Space Shuttle Program

Village Earth Press
Vestal, New York 13850
www.villageearthpress.com

First Printing
9 8 7 6 5 4 3 2 1

Series ISBN (paperback): 978-1-62524-444-4
ISBN (paperback): 978-1-62524-402-4
ebook ISBN: 978-1-62524-037-8

Library of Congress Control Number: 2014931522

Author: Etingoff, Kim.

Contents

Chapter 1: Early Exploration 7

Chapter 2: Famous Missions 21

Chapter 3: The *Challenger* Disaster 31

Chapter 4: Retirement and Beyond 43

Here's What We Recommend 54

Index 55

About the Author & Picture Credits 56

ONE

Early Exploration

Outer space fascinates us. Young people and adults alike wonder what's out there. They imagine what it would be like to explore space.

For a very few people, outer space isn't only something they dream about. They really get to launch into space. Some people have even walked on the moon!

All that exploration has happened partly because of space shuttles. For thirty years, space shuttles in the United States took astronauts from Earth up to space. Before that, other spacecraft brought the first people into space.

Today, the American space shuttle program is *retired*. But that doesn't mean we're not still exploring space. And even though the space shuttles are retired now, scientists learned many important things from them.

This picture of Buzz Aldrin's bootprint in the dust on the moon's surface has become an important part of the world's history.

Why Space?

People have been curious about outer space for a long time. Thousands of years ago, people looked up at the sky and gave names to the stars and planets. They made calendars based on the movements of the sun, moon, and stars.

When something has been **retired**, it is no longer used for work.

Technology is made up of all the scientific tools and machines people have invented.

Missions are tasks, like having a man walk on the moon, that people want to see happen.

As time went on, people learned more and more about the region beyond the Earth's atmosphere. But no one had ever actually flown into outer space.

In the twentieth century, human beings finally had enough *technology* to start thinking about sending people into space. People knew that if we could enter space, we could learn all sorts of things.

We could learn about how the Earth, the solar system, and even the entire universe work. We might even discover life somewhere else in the universe. A lot of work had to be done, though, before we could send a person into space.

Finally, we did send people into space. We have learned a lot about the universe from those space *missions*. But we still have a lot left to learn!

A **satellite** is something that travels around and around a larger thing in space.

When two people, teams, or countries are **competing**, they are each trying to do better than the other.

The First Missions

The very first *satellite* sent into space was called *Sputnik I*. *Sputnik* was a very small satellite the Soviet Union launched in 1957.

The United States was *competing* with Soviet Union in the 1950s. Both countries wanted to be the most powerful nation in the world. The Soviets successfully sent the first satellite in the world into space, but the United States wanted to be the best at space exploration. Americans wanted to keep up with the Soviets.

One year later, Americans launched their own satellite called the *Explorer I*. About the same time, the U.S. government decided it wanted to do still more. The country needed a program to focus on space exploration. The American government set up the National Aeronautics and Space Administration (NASA).

The Sputnik Satellites

Sputnik I, the first human-made satellite in space, was very tiny. It was about the size of a basketball and weighed 184 pounds—about as much as an adult man. *Sputnik I* circled the Earth in 98 minutes. A month later, the Soviet Union launched *Sputnik II* into space. That time, the satellite was big enough to hold a dog. Laika the dog was the first Earth creature to enter space!

Starting in 1958, NASA was in charge of all the American space programs. At first, NASA sent up satellites that took pictures of the moon and did other experiments in space.

Yuri Gagarin's trip to outer space made him famous throughout the world.

People in Space

Only a couple years after the Soviets launched the first satellite into space, they sent up the very first person. In 1961, Yuri Gagarin became the first human being in space.

Gagarin spent almost two hours circling our planet in the spacecraft *Vostok I*. He looked out of the windows into space and down at Earth. He had lots of equipment with him, but scientists and engineers on Earth controlled the *Vostok I*. After his two-hour voyage, Gagarin landed safely, proving that people really could fly in space.

Then, in 1961, the United States sent up the second person. Astronaut Alan Shepard spent just a few minutes in space. However, he controlled the whole flight himself. He safely launched his spacecraft into space and came back with lots of new scientific information.

The next year, John Glenn became the first American to **orbit** our planet in space. He

> To **orbit** means to travel around and around something in a circle.
>
> **Extravehicular** means "outside a vehicle."

went up in the *Friendship 7*, and then he went around the Earth three times in about five hours. After he returned, people treated him as though he were a hero. Today, he is one of the most famous astronauts in the world.

NASA wanted to do more than just send people up to orbit the planet. They wanted to land people on the moon!

The first step was figuring out how to have people perform spacewalks. Spacewalks are also called **extravehicular** activity, or EVA. The people who had gone into space had stayed in their spacecraft. Scientists weren't sure yet they could safely send people outside of the spacecraft.

Once again, the Soviets were the first to reach the new goal. In 1965, Alexei Leonov was the first person to do a spacewalk. Leonov left the *Voshkod 2* and floated in space for about twenty minutes. He was tied to the spacecraft of course! Otherwise he would have floated off into space.

A couple of months later, the first American to do a spacewalk was Ed White. He spent a half hour floating outside the *Gemini 4* mission. When he was ordered to go back to the spacecraft, he said, "It's the saddest moment of my life." He wasn't ready to go back inside!

Space Suits

Scientists had to make sure astronauts doing space-walks were safe. Humans can't survive without suits in space, because there isn't any oxygen in space. This means people can't breathe, but it also means that there's no air pushing against their bodies in space. The lack of air pressure is very dangerous to human bodies. Special suits, however, keep astronauts safe and able to breath. On the very first spacewalk, Alexei Leonov's spacesuit almost didn't work, though. During his time floating in space, his suit got bigger because the pressure inside the suit made it blow up like a balloon. He found he was too big to fit back into the entry to the spacecraft! He ended up letting enough air out of his suit so he could fit through the door. Then he safely returned to Earth.

Apollo Missions

NASA was ready to do even more. The scientists at NASA had learned how to launch people safely into space. They knew how to have them

Apollo 11 *launches with a Saturn V rocket, the largest and most powerful type of rocket ever used.*

THE SPACE SHUTTLE PROGRAM

safely leave their spacecraft. Next, they had to figure out how to land them on the moon.

NASA came up with the Apollo mission program. In the years that followed, NASA would launch several missions, all called Apollo. The goal was to land one of those missions on the moon. These missions had other goals, too. NASA wanted to show that the United States was the most powerful country in the world when it came to space exploration. The Apollo missions would also be able to collect **data** about the moon, which would lead to new discoveries.

The Apollo missions' ships didn't look like the space shuttles we've seen lately. They had three parts. The first was called the command module or CM. The CM had areas for the crew to live and to fly the spacecraft. The second part was called the service module or SM. The SM had a lot of computer equipment to fly the spacecraft. It also had the engines for moving the spacecraft. The third part was the lunar module or LM. This part took two crewmembers to the moon and then brought them back to the main part of the spacecraft. All together, the three parts took astronauts thousands of miles from Earth, to the moon, and back again.

The spacecraft were launched into space on the ends of rockets, but once they were high enough, they broke off from the rockets. When the spacecraft returned, they splashed into the oceans, where people were waiting to pick up the astronauts.

The first few missions didn't send people into space. But they were getting ready to send people out into space. They tested different parts of the spacecraft to make sure they would work right. *Apollo 7* was the first Apollo mission to send humans up. There were ten more Apollo flights with people on them.

Famous Words

Apollo 11 was aired on TV for audiences all over the world. People watched in awe as Neil Armstrong first stepped on the moon and said, "One small step for man, one giant leap for mankind." Today, lots of people have heard these words. They express how far technology and science have brought humans.

Data is scientific information that is gathered during an experiment.

Astronaut Alan Bean records footage for study during the Apollo 12 mission.

Apollo 8 carried the first people around the moon. The spacecraft circled the moon ten times. Images from the spacecraft were sent to Earth, where people watched them on TV. This was the first time anyone had seen an "earthrise"—the Earth rising over the moon's horizon.

In 1969, *Apollo 11* landed the first person on the moon. NASA had accomplished one if its most important goals! Astronauts Neil Armstrong and Buzz Aldrin spent two and a half hours on the moon, collecting things to take back to Earth.

Switch to Shuttles

After *Apollo 17*, some people wanted to continue space exploration. They wanted to create space colonies on the moon, or send astronauts to Mars or beyond.

However, NASA didn't have enough money to keep doing expensive programs like the Apollo missions. And people were a little less interested in space exploration than they had been. After all, they had landed a person on the moon!

NASA ended the Apollo program and began the space shuttle program. Space shuttles looked a little like planes. They were big and were sent into space by rocket boosters. When they returned to Earth, they landed on runways, like airplanes. They were called shuttles because they would bring astronauts from Earth to space and back again, a little like a shuttle bus that carries people from one place and back.

NASA designed the space shuttles to be used over and over (instead of just once, the way the Apollo spacecraft had been). This

Americans and Soviets Working Together

For a long time, the United States and the Soviet Union were in a "space race." They were competing to see who could send the most people into space and develop the best technologies. After the United States became the first country to land a person on the moon, though, the two countries started working together. After the Apollo program, NASA and the Soviet Union started the Apollo-Soyuz Test Project. In 1975, a spacecraft from the United States and a spacecraft from the Soviet Union met in space. The crews visited each spacecraft and worked together. Today, the United States and Russia (which used to be the main part of the Soviet Union) continue to work together in space.

The Soyuz spacecraft, built by Russia, was used during joint missions between Russia and the United States. Today, Soyuz spacecraft are still used to bring people up to the International Space Station.

would help save money. Space shuttle missions also lasted a lot longer than the Apollo missions. Astronauts were in space for one or two weeks, instead of just a few hours or days. In addition, astronauts would do experiments in space. They would also build and go to space stations.

Space stations are large structures that float in space and are meant to stay up there for a long time. Today, astronauts travel to space stations to perform experiments in space. They live there for months, sometimes even over a year.

Several space stations have orbited Earth. The Soviet Union launched the first space station, Salyut. The United States later launched Skylab. Today, astronauts work on the International Space Station, along with a space station launched by China. Space shuttles were a key part of building and running these space stations.

Find Out Even More

You can learn a lot from a book like the one you have in your hands right now—but a book like this one only has so many pages. Only so much information can fit inside it. The author had to choose which information was important to include—and which information to leave out. Reading this book is a good way to start to learn about space shuttles and space exploration, but there's a lot more information out there you could learn.

If you want to find even more, there are a few things you could do. A first step might be to go to your school library or the public library. The list of books here gives you titles you can look for in the card catalog. Or you could ask the librarian to help you. Even if your library doesn't have all these books, you'll be able to find the section where there are other books like these.

Koestler-Grack, Rachel A. *Space Shuttle Columbia Disaster.* Minneapolis,Minn.: Abdo Publishing Company, 2004.

Sexton, Collen. *Space Shuttles.* Minneapolis, Minn.: Bellwether Media, 2010.

Wallace, Karen. *Rockets and Spaceships.* New York: DK Publishing, 2011.

Zuehlke, Jeffrey. *The Space Shuttle.* Minneapolis, Minn.: Lerner Publications Company, 2007.

Then look through each of the books. Check out the table of contents at the front of the book. Leaf through the pages. Ask yourself these questions:

- Does it look like this book will give me information that I didn't get from the book I just read about space shuttles?
- Can I read and understand this book? Maybe it's a higher reading level than what you're used to. You might want to give it a try anyway. After reading this book, you'll be familiar with some of the terminology. You'll be able to stretch your mind—and while you're learning about space shuttles, you'll be improving your reading skills.
- How is the material organized? Will I be able to easily look up information I want to understand—or will I need to read the entire book to grasp what the book has to offer? Does the book have an index where I can look up what interests me? Does it have headings on each page that break down the information?

    You may *want* to read the entire book anyway, but if you just want to locate a particular piece of information—for instance, how old was John Glenn when he first went into space?—then things like indexes and page headings will help you locate the information quickly.
- Does the book have photographs and other images that help me understand this topic better? You don't *need* images to learn about space travel, but they may help you better understand what this amazing technology looks like and how it works.

TWO

Famous Missions

The very first space shuttle was launched in 1981. In the thirty years that the space shuttle program existed, the United States built five space shuttles.

Altogether, the five shuttles flew 135 missions. Astronauts on the missions did countless scientific experiments. For example, they sent images of space back to Earth for people to see. Space shuttles made world news over and over, sometimes for exciting reasons of discovery—and sometimes for disasters.

Enterprise

The first space shuttle was called the *Enterprise*. It wasn't quite a real space shuttle. NASA built it to test the space shuttle program. The *Enterprise* looked like a space shuttle, and it could fly. However, it couldn't actually make the trip to space.

The Enterprise *was named after the fictional* U.S.S. Enterprise, *a starship in the 1960s TV series* Star Trek. *Although the* Enterprise *never went into space, it still played an important part in the space shuttle program.*

NASA started testing the *Enterprise* in 1977. First, the shuttle flew attached to a plane. Soon after, the Enterprise flew on its own, though still within the Earth's atmosphere.

After the tests, NASA thought about making *Enterprise* a real space shuttle. Rebuilding it would be too expensive, though, so instead NASA used parts from the *Enterprise* to build other shuttles. The rest of the shuttle was eventually given to the Smithsonian Museum in Washington, D.C.

Columbia

The first real space shuttle was *Columbia*. *Columbia* weighed 4.5 million pounds and carried people on board.

The first time *Columbia* went into space, everything went well. Astronauts John Young and Bob Crippen had a successful mission and a safe return to Earth.

The *Columbia's* voyage marked a lot of "firsts" in space exploration. It was the first time a new program was launched with a person on board. All the first flights of past missions—like the Apollo program—were unmanned.

One *Columbia* mission in 1983 was designed for people to do science experiments. That flight was the first time Spacelab was used. Spacelab was a laboratory on board the shuttle that contained equipment for performing experiments. The crew spent ten days doing experiments in space. Spacelab was used on more than twenty other space shuttle missions after that.

Unfortunately, *Columbia's* story came to an end in 2003. On its twenty-eighth mission, the shuttle broke apart as it was coming in to land. All seven astronauts on board were killed. (The end of chapter 3 will tell you more about the *Columbia* disaster.)

Challenger

The second space shuttle was *Challenger*, which first flew in 1983.

Challenger made a lot of news headlines. For example, astronauts on the *Challenger* were the first to repair a satellite and return it to orbit.

Space Shuttle Parts

Space shuttles were very complicated. One shuttle had about 2.5 million moving parts! Here are a few of the biggest parts in a space shuttle:

- Orbiter vehicle: the part of the shuttle that looks like a plane. This is the only part that actually went into space.
- Solid rocket boosters: these helped get the space shuttle off the ground during the first two minutes after liftoff.
- External fuel tank: this contained the fuel that got the space shuttle off the ground and into space. It eventually separated from the orbiter. The fuel tank is the only part of the shuttle that wasn't reused.
- Space shuttle main engines: these also helped get the shuttle into space, and then they continued to work for a few minutes after the rocket boosters separated.

In addition, the first American woman in space went up in *Challenger*. Sally Ride went on the second *Challenger* mission in 1983. She and four other astronauts brought up two satellites to release into space. Up to that point, NASA had only allowed men on board any spacecraft. The first woman in space was Soviet Valentina Tereshkova, who went in 1963. But no American women had gone into space before Sally Ride.

The first African American in space, Guion Bluford, went up on the next *Challenger* mission, with four other astronauts. They did some experiments and released a satellite. Then they safely returned home.

Sadly, *Challenger* also ended in disaster, when it exploded after takeoff in 1986. (Chapter 3 will tell you more about this.)

Discovery

NASA's third shuttle was *Discovery*, which first flew in 1984. Out of the five shuttles, *Discovery* flew the most missions.

Discovery was the first shuttle to fly after the Challenger disaster. Everyone in the world watched the launch on TV. NASA worked hard to make sure nothing went wrong—and nothing did. The crew on the *Discovery* released a satellite and did experiments, much like other successful missions.

The view from Discovery *of the moon setting behind the Earth.*

In 1990, another *Discovery* crew launched the Hubble Space Telescope. NASA wanted to put a telescope in space so it could take clear pictures of stars, galaxies, and other things in space. *Discovery* brought the telescope into space, and five astronauts got it working. We still use the Hubble Space Telescope today.

In addition to its many missions, *Discovery* and its crew tested out new safety procedures that NASA created after the *Challenger* disaster to make sure astronauts stayed safe.

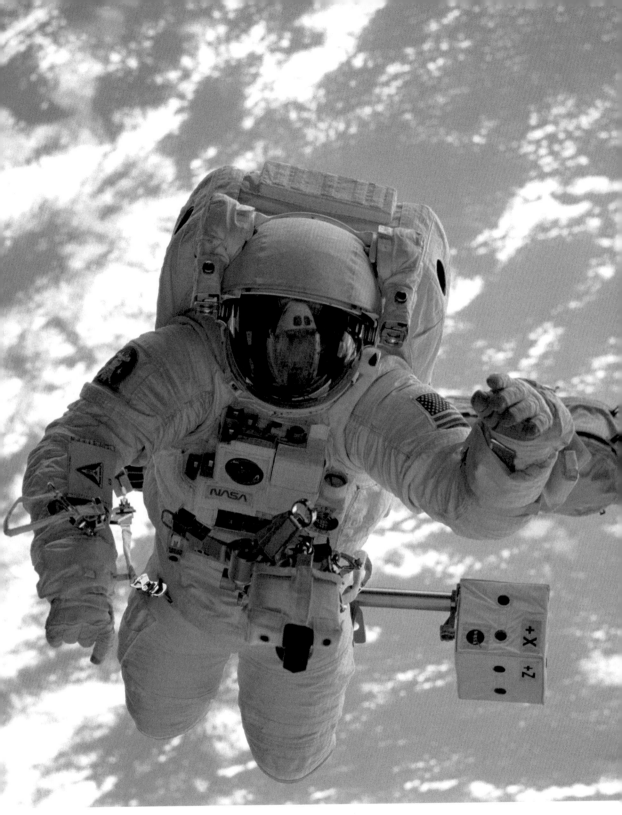

Astronaut Michael Gernhardt conducts repairs from outside the shuttle. You can see the space shuttle Endeavor *reflected in his visor.*

Atlantis

The fourth space shuttle was *Atlantis*. Like the other shuttles, *Atlantis* did some important scientific work. Instruments were sent from Atlantis to Jupiter and Venus to collect information from even farther out in the solar system.

After many missions, *Atlantis* flew the last shuttle mission ever. In 2011, four astronauts brought lots of supplies to the International Space Station. When *Atlantis* returned to Earth, the space shuttle missions were over. (Chapter 4 will tell you more about the end of the shuttle missions.)

Endeavour

The last shuttle built was *Endeavour*. NASA built this shuttle to replace the Challenger, because scientists wanted to make sure they had enough shuttles to send into space continuously.

In 1998, *Endeavour* brought the first American parts to the International Space Station. At the time, Russia was just beginning to build the space station. Many more shuttle missions brought up more parts. Today, the space station is complete, thanks in part to shuttles like *Endeavour*.

Find Out Even More

Reading a book is a great way to discover more about space shuttles. When you read a book like this one, the author has already done most of the work for you. She's taken all the information and organized it for you. She's broken it up in chunks and put it in order so you can understand it more easily.

Using the Internet is also a great way to learn more about space shuttles. There's no limit to the amount of information that can be stored on the Internet, so you may be able to find out more if you search there than you would from any book like this one. The only problem is—you'll have to be able to organize the information yourself! You'll have to go looking for it and pull it out of the enormous web of information that makes up the Internet.

Here's how you get started. First, you come up with key words. These are important words that have to do with your topic. When you do an Internet search, these are the words you'll enter into the search engine (like Google, for example, or Bing) in order to call up websites that have to do with that topic.

So if you look back over the two chapters that you've read so far in this book, you'll be able to make a list of key words. Here are some examples.

space shuttle
Yuri Gagarin
Apollo

NASA
Alan Shepard
space station

Enterprise
Challenger
Atlantis

Columbia
Discovery
Sally Ride

Type any of these words into the search engine, and you'll find lots of sites to choose from!

THREE

The *Challenger* Disaster

The history of space exploration is filled with lots of **triumphs** and discoveries. Unfortunately, it also has a couple of disasters.

The first big space exploration disaster was the explosion of the *Challenger* space shuttle in 1986. All seven astronauts on the shuttle died, an entire shuttle was lost, and the space program in the United States changed forever.

Triumphs are great wins.

How It Happened

Challenger was the second space shuttle built by NASA. For nine missions, it had gone into space and come back without any serious problems.

Then, on the tenth mission, just 73 seconds after lifting off, the shuttle exploded over the Atlantic Ocean.

If the temperature outside a spacecraft on the launch pad drops too much, pipes can freeze and burst. This can damage the craft and force mission control to cancel the launch.

Thousands of people were watching from the ground in Cape Canaveral, Florida, where NASA's shuttles were launched. And many more people were watching on their TVs at home. Students were watching in schools around the world. Everyone was stunned as they watched the shuttle explode. Viewers' excitement turned into horror.

What happened? It took NASA two years to figure it out.

NASA collected all the **debris** they could find from the shuttle. The government also put together a **commission** to look into what happened. Several astronauts served on the commission.

The weather played a big part in causing the explosion. *Challenger* launched in January, and it was cold, even for Florida—below freezing. At the time, scientists were worried about some of the shuttle's parts. They thought the parts might not work right in the cold.

That's what the commission found, too. Certain parts that held together one of the rocket boosters on the shuttle had failed. They weren't made to work in such cold temperatures. When the parts, called O-rings, broke, hydrogen gas started leaking from the shuttle. Then, the shuttle started breaking apart.

The commission also found that communication within NASA wasn't very good. The right people hadn't heard the scientists' worries about the cold. If they had, NASA might have decided not to launch the shuttle until the weather was warmer.

Finally, the commission found that NASA scientists were working too fast

Debris is the bits and pieces that have fallen off of an object.

Commissions are written permissions and commands to look into events.

The Crew

Seven people were on board *Challenger* when it exploded—six astronauts and one teacher. Teacher Christa McAuliffe was chosen as the first non-astronaut to go into space. She was picked from thousands of teachers who applied. Then she had some training to get her ready. She was planning on teaching some lessons from space, to promote young people's interest in the space program. Her crewmates were commander Francis Scobee; pilot Mike Smith; missions specialists Judy Resnik, Ron McNair, and Ellison Onizuka; and payload specialist Greg Jarvis.

After the Challenger *disaster, NASA was faced with the task of collecting the remains of the exploded shuttle and trying to figure out what went wrong.*

The Challenger *crewmembers whose lives were lost. In the back row from left to right: Mission Specialist, Ellison S. Onizuka, Teacher in Space Participant Sharon Christa McAuliffe, Payload Specialist, Greg Jarvis and Mission Specialist, Judy Resnik. In the front row from left to right: Pilot Mike Smith, Commander, Dick Scobee and Mission Specialist, Ron McNair.*

and too hard. NASA was sending up a lot of shuttle missions. But the work was too much for the number of people at NASA.

What Happened After

The *Challenger* disaster changed how NASA ran the space shuttle program. Everyone wanted to avoid another explosion. NASA figured out how to solve its problems before sending up another shuttle.

On the evening of the Challenger *disaster, President Ronald Reagan spoke to the American people from the White House. He ended his speech with the famous words: "The crew of the space shuttle* Challenger *honored us by the manner in which they lived their lives. We will never forget them, nor the last time we saw them, this morning, as they prepared for the journey and waved goodbye and 'slipped the surly bonds of earth' to 'touch the face of God.'"*

THE SPACE SHUTTLE PROGRAM

People were also angry. Many people had been watching on TV and from the ground, and they had seen the shuttle explode. Lots of students in schools had been watching, because one of the crewmembers was a teacher.

In response, NASA stopped the space shuttle program for almost three years. Instead of sending shuttles into space, they focused on fixing the problems with the shuttle and within the NASA organization. They created a new Office of Safety, Reliability, and Quality Assurance. The people in that department made sure the shuttle and astronauts were safe before and during flight. Engineers redesigned the solid rocket boosters, the part that had failed on the *Challenger*. NASA made the workload more manageable in the shuttle program. Shuttles would stop bringing up satellites. NASA would use other spacecraft to do that. And shuttles wouldn't have to be launched as often. Plus, since NASA had lost a shuttle, scientists and engineers built a new one, the *Endeavour*.

In 1988, NASA restarted the shuttle program. *Discovery* was sent into space, and for another twenty-five years, shuttles were much safer.

But people thought about NASA differently now from what they had before. Before, they trusted NASA. NASA had sent people to the moon! But now, people were worried. They had learned that space exploration could be dangerous.

The Next Disaster

In 2003, another space shuttle disaster happened. *Columbia* broke apart as it was returning to Earth from a mission. This time, seven astronauts died.

A team of people looked at what went wrong with the shuttle and within NASA. This time, they found that a piece of *Columbia* broke off as the shuttle was launching. The piece hit another part of the shuttle that protected it from heat when it came back to Earth. Most of the mission then went as planned. But when *Columbia* reentered the Earth's atmosphere, the heat damaged the shuttle where that original piece had hit it, and the shuttle broke apart.

The space shuttle Columbia *launches, shortly before the disaster that lead to the deaths of seven more astronauts.*

The team found that many of the same problems that had led to the *Challenger* disaster had caused this one. Some people at NASA had seen the damage to the shuttle, and they had talked about it. But no one decided to do anything. And again, NASA tried to fix the problems. However, NASA didn't have much time to try out their new plans. Soon after the *Columbia* disaster, the shuttle program ended.

Find Out Even More

When you type a key word into a search engine, you'll find that lots of sites come up. With so much information to choose from, you might feel overwhelmed. Say you do a search using the word "NASA." How do you sort through all the sites that come up?

If you use Google as your search engine, here are the sites you might see, starting from the top:

- The official site for NASA: www.nasa.gov.
- A news article about NASA. These will probably change from day to day, depending on what's happening in the world.
- A Wikipedia article about NASA: en.wikipedia.org/wiki/NASA.
- The visitors' information site for the Johnson Space Center at NASA: spacecenter.org.
- The National Auto Sport Association site: www.nasaproracing.com.
- The NASA YouTube site, where you can watch video clips about NASA's program: www.youtube.com/user/NASAtelevision.

And all that's just on the first page! Google has more than 200 million other sites you could look at. But for now, take a look at what' s on this first page. You can already start to sort through it just with a quick glance.

There's one site on the list that you shouldn't bother clicking on, because it has nothing do with the space program. It's not the right NASA! Which site is that?

There's another site that has to do with the right NASA, but it probably won't have the kind of information you're looking for. Unless you're planning to visit the Johnson Space Center and do some hands-on research, the information at the visitors' site won't be that helpful to you.

That leaves NASA's official site, the news articles, the Wikipedia article, and the YouTube site. Of those four site, which do you think is the most reliable and will have the most information to offer? Why?

FOUR

Retirement and Beyond

The space shuttle program came to an end in 2011. Thirty years after the first shuttle flew into space, the last one landed on Earth.

Although the shuttles had done a lot of important scientific work, it was time for them to retire. But why?

Reasons for Retirement

One of the reasons for bringing an end to the space shuttle program was that it had accomplished its goals. One goal had been to build a space station, which had happened. The International Space Station was up in space and working.

A second reason was that the space shuttles were getting old. Each had flown a lot of missions. They cost a lot to fix. And if NASA wanted to

This picture, taken from the space shuttle Discovery, *shows the International Space Station during one of the early stages of its construction.*

keep the shuttle program going, they would have to build new shuttles.

The third reason was that the shuttle program had experienced two big disasters. No one wanted things like that to happen ever again, but it would cost NASA a lot of time and money to fix the problems that had caused those disasters. NASA decided to focus on other things instead.

In 2004, President George W. Bush made the decision to stop sending shuttles into space. NASA had a few years before it had to retire the shuttles, though, so the shuttles helped finish building the International Space Station.

After that, in 2011, each of the three remaining shuttles made a final journey. *Discovery* was the first shuttle to officially retire. It successfully finished its final mission in March 2011. Next, *Endeavour* flew its last mission on June 1. And *Atlantis* flew the last shuttle flight ever in July of that year.

The International Space Station

Right now, the main reason people go in space is to visit and live on the International Space Station (ISS). People started building it in 1998, and they finished in 2011. Astronauts go to the ISS to do experiments in biology, physics, astronomy, and more. Astronauts from more than a dozen countries have flown to the ISS. They work together in space to discover as much as they can. The organizations that keep the ISS working—like NASA—plan to use the ISS until at least 2020 and possibly even longer.

Retirement Homes

NASA didn't take the shuttles apart or put them in storage. Instead, it gave the three remaining shuttles to organizations across the United States, so people could see them. *Discovery* was given to the Smithsonian National Air and Space Museum in Washington, D.C. *Atlantis* was put on display at the Kennedy Space Center in Florida. *Endeavour* was given to the California Science Center in Los Angeles.

Now people could visit the shuttles up close. Visitors to these museums can see what the shuttles look like and learn about how they worked and what discoveries astronauts made while on board.

United States

As the space shuttle Atlantis is retired, fireworks celebrate the many years that these ships brought us a little closer to the stars.

THE SPACE SHUTTLE PROGRAM

Astronauts on the International Space Station always have a view of home from the windows in the Station's Cupola.

Space Travel Now

Astronauts are still going into space, but they don't use American shuttles to get there. Astronauts from the United States go up on Russian spacecraft to the International Space Station to conduct experiments.

The United States has to pay Russia to have the astronauts go up to space. But it's cheaper to buy "seats" into space than to run the shuttle program! Until the United States has another spacecraft in which to send people up, American astronauts will have to use other countries' spacecraft.

The Field Integrated Design and Operations (FIDO) rover will never go to space, but it is used here on Earth to study what driving conditions will be like on Mars. Here, it studies rock samples collected in the southwestern United States.

People who want to go to space have another option today. In the past, governments were in charge of space exploration. For example, NASA is a government-run organization. However, now there are companies, run by individuals, sending people into space. These companies hope to send trained astronauts. They also want to sell tickets to ordinary people who just want to go into space for the adventure.

When people are **researching** something, they are finding out more about it. Research can be done by reading books, by talking with people, and by doing experiments.

An **asteroid** is a small, rocky object that orbits the sun.

In fact, Russia has already offered places for "space tourists" on board their Soyuz spacecraft. Several wealthy people have already gone to space, paying anywhere from $20 million to $40 million each!

The Future

For a while after the shuttles retired, people argued about what would happen next. President Bush wanted to send people back to the moon and eventually to Mars.

NASA started a new project called Constellation to replace the shuttle program. The plan was to build new spacecraft that would bring people to the International Space Station. After that, NASA would send people back to the moon, and then to Mars.

But when Barack Obama became president, he asked scientists to take another look at the plan. The scientists said the Constellation program didn't have enough money. NASA was behind schedule. Constellation wasn't working.

President Obama cancelled Constellation and came up with new goals for the American space program. NASA would now start *researching* and building a rocket for deep space travel, one that would go further out into space, beyond where astronauts had gone in shuttles. The plan was to send people to an *asteroid*. After that, they would go to Mars and beyond.

The space shuttle program may be over, but with many other projects in the works, the future of space exploration looks bright!

Today no one knows what exactly is in store for space exploration. What will replace the space shuttles? Will humans ever land on Mars?

During the thirty years of the space shuttle program, we learned a lot about space. Many people believe we could learn more if we continue to explore space.

People never imagined what would happen when they sent the first satellite into space. In just a few short years, they sent a human being into space, then landed on the moon. And after that, they regularly sent crews of people into space on shuttles.

Who knows what will come next!

Find Out Even More

If you're looking online for more information about space shuttles and space exploration, here are some things to keep in mind:

- Remember that just because something is on the Internet, that doesn't necessarily mean it's true. Different people make different kinds of websites—and some websites will be better than others.
- Think about how reliable the site you're using is. "Reliable" means you can depend on that site to give you information that's true and up-to-date. For example, Wikipedia sites are often great places to start when you're doing research on the Internet—but you should never depend on Wikipedia being 100 percent accurate and reliable. All the information on Wikipedia has been put there by users who have put all their knowledge together into one spot. It's a really cool thing that so many people could work together, without getting paid, to make such an amazing collection of information—but there could be mistakes in the information. You should always check anything you learn from Wikimedia against a more reliable source. At the end of every Wikimedia article is usually a heading called "External Links." Sometimes there's also a heading called "Further Reading." Lists like these are great ways to find the best sites on whatever topic you're searching.

- Here are some questions to ask yourself that will help you judge how reliable the site is:

Who made the site? If a university or a government organization, for example, created the site, then chances are good that the people who made the site were very careful to include only information they know is true. But if a student made the site as a school project, the information it contains may not be as good.

Why did they make the site? If the site's purpose is to teach people, then it's more likely to be true. But if the site is intended to get people to buy something, then the information may not be as accurate.

When did they make the site? You can't always tell, but often, websites will indicate the last date they were updated. If you can see that a website hasn't been touched for the past three years, then it probably contains information that is out-of-date. New things will have happened since then that may have changed the entire story.

What's their point of view? Everyone looks at the world a little differently because we each have our own points of view. A woman might look at a certain set of facts differently from what a man would; a young person might view information differently from what an older person would; a person in Africa might see things differently from a person in North America. This doesn't mean that the information will be *wrong*. It just means that different people may choose to include or emphasize some information over another, because it seems more important to them. If you know their perspective (their point of view), then you'll be able to judge their website better.

Here's What We Recommend

If you want to use the Internet to learn more about space shuttles and space exploration, here are some good sites to get you started!

Astronomy for Kids: Space Shuttle
www.kidsastronomy.com/space_shuttle.htm

Kids Discover Magazine: Space Exploration
www.kidsdiscover.com/space-exploration-for-kids

Kids Life In Space
www.esa.int/esaKIDSen/SEMT0EBE8JG_LifeinSpace_0.html

NASA
www.nasa.gov

NASA Kids Club
www.nasa.gov/audience/forkids/kidsclub/flash/index.html

A Rare Peek Inside Space Shuttle Discovery
www.dogonews.com/2011/6/28/a-rare-peek-inside-space-shuttlediscovery

Index

Aldrin, Buzz 8, 15
Apollo 11–15, 23, 28
Armstrong, Neil 13, 15
astronauts 7, 11, 13, 15, 17, 21, 23–25, 27, 31, 33, 37–38, 45, 47, 49
Atlantis 27, 29, 45–46

Bluford, Guion 24
Bush, George W. 45, 49

Challenger 23–25, 27, 29, 31, 33–37, 39
Columbia 18, 23, 29, 37–39
Constellation 49

disasters 21, 31, 45
Discovery 21, 24–25, 29, 37, 44–45

Earth 7–11, 13, 15, 17, 21, 23, 25, 27, 36–37, 43, 48
Endeavour 27, 37, 45
Enterprise 21–23, 29
experiments 9, 15, 17, 21, 23–24, 45, 47, 49

future 49–50

Gagarin, Yuri 10, 28
Glenn, John 10, 19

Hubble Space Telescope 24–25

International Space Station 16–17, 27, 43–45, 47, 49

Kennedy Space Center 45

Leonov, Alexei 11

Mars 15, 48–49, 51
McAuliffe, Christa 33, 35
missions 8–9, 11, 13, 15–16, 21, 23–25, 27, 31, 33, 35, 43
moon 7–9, 11, 13, 15, 25, 37, 49, 51

NASA 9, 11, 13, 15, 21, 23–25, 27–28, 31, 33–35, 37, 39–41, 43, 45, 49

Obama, Barack 49

retirement 43, 45
Ride, Sally 24, 29
rockets 13, 18
Russia 15–16, 27, 47, 49

safety 25, 37
satellites 9, 24, 37
scientists 7, 10–11, 27, 33, 37, 49
Shepard, Alan 10, 28
Smithsonian museum 23
Soviet Union 9, 15, 17
space 7–11, 13, 15–19, 21–28, 31, 33, 35–38, 40–41, 43–52
spacewalks 11
space stations 15, 17
Sputnik 9
stars 8, 25, 46

technology 8, 13, 19
Tereshkova, Valentina 24
TV 13, 22, 24, 37

White, Ed 11, 36

About the Author

Kim Etingoff lives in Boston, Massachusetts, spending part of her time working on farms. Kim writes educational books for young people on topics including health, science, history, and more.

Picture Credits

Made in the USA
Lexington, KY
07 April 2018